Dr. Paul's TOTAL Relief

Depression
Formulas that BLAST the pain

Book 1

Dr. Paul's TOTAL Relief Systems

Book 1

Depression

Formulas that BLAST the pain…FAST!

Dr. Paul Joseph Young

© *Copyright 2015 by Dr. Paul Joseph Young*

No part of this book can be reproduced in any form apart from the consent of the author. Short parts may be used in a review.

Cover page photo from free art source number 1211428_77489127

A **TOTAL RELIEF** *SYSTEMS* **publication**

All my books are written in a conversational, informal style on purpose. Formality too often bores. I don't want you to get distracted while reading this book. I want you to finish it, learn from it, and live the truth out in your life. My desire, more than anything, is to help you find TOTAL RELIEF from your depression.

You will also find the formatting of the paragraphs and sentences are arranged differently than most other books. This makes it easy to read, easy to get the principles, and most of all will help you to blast through your depression and find the joy you deserve.

Bravo!

This book is not intended to replace any kind of therapy you are presently taking. ALWAYS TALK WITH YOUR DOCTOR or therapist before making any radical changes. And DO NOT stop taking your medication. Until you have worked through all three books and learned how to apply my unique program, then, and only then, should you talk with your therapist or doctor to see if you can either stop or reduce your medications.

In this book I write about many depressed people whom I have counseled. The stories are true, but have been disguised enough to protect the identity of those who have overcome their depression. Some stories have been blended with other accounts so that the confidentiality of my true clients can be protected. In all, I have worked with thousands who have taken my unique formulas and have found new and transformed lives, for which I am thankful.

TABLE OF CONTENTS

Introduction

- Why this book will change your life.
- Reasons why you MUST read this book.
- My EDUCATION and EXPERIENCE equips me to help you, now.
- I don't just give some of the answers, I give ALL of the answers you are looking for.

Chapter 1

BREAKTHROUGH FORMULA 1

Chapter 2 - THE KEY...

that unlocks the door of depression

Chapter 3 - Another KEY...
that helps to get you out of depression

Chapter 4

BREAKTHROUGH FORMULA 2

Dramatically increasing the effectiveness of Formula 1

1) The false, generally accepted formula that many accept and believe – to their detriment
2) The breakthrough, true formula, Formula 2, and why it is so effective in blasting through depression
3) How to use Formula 2
4) Real life stories

Chapter 5

BREAKTHROUGH FORMULA 3

How this brings everything together

1) The Breakthrough formula that will set you free form

your prison of depression
2) How to use this formula to break loose from your hopelessness
3) Real life stories
4) A summation of the three formulas and how they will help you blast through your depression

APPENDIX A

Review of the three breakthrough formulas

APPENDIX B

A description of the various forms of therapy for depression and why my breakthrough formulas are superior

APPENDIX C

Why using the power of positive thinking and affirmations to rid depression often do not work

INTRODUCTION

A MESSAGE FROM

DR. PAUL

My Dear Reader,

This is NOT just another book on depression and definitely not your typical self-help book. Nor is it just some kind of pop psychology.

No way!

I take your depression seriously.

You see, depression has been referred to as the number one health problem in the world. If not treated, it can kill. But don't be afraid.

MY APPROACH

My approach to help you goes incredibly beyond what most programs and books offer. In my opinion, almost all texts on depression, even the best sellers, fall short of what you desperately seek. They render some relief, but most of them do not deliver to you the healing and freedom you desire. They do not take you all the way to TOTAL RELIEF.

How many times have you picked up a book or had a therapy session that gave you hope. You experienced some improvement from your depression. But there it is again, raising its ugly head. Your meds aren't working the way they used to, you continue to go to therapy and read books, on and on and on, hoping, to have a breakthrough. Now you pick up my book. It looks different. And you see the title, TOTAL RELIEF.

TOTAL!

That's what you're looking for. Your heart desperately seeks to put your depression behind you…once and for all.

Well, my friend, you have come to the right place.

My promise to you is this:

You will be taken on a journey that will *not just get rid of your PAIN, but the ROOT CAUSE of your pain,* restoring you to the person you were meant to be.

Quite a promise, isn't it!

FOOLS GOLD

Recently, I surveyed over 500 books on the market, looking at their systems, their promises, assurances and even guarantees. They all had a plan to help you get rid of your depression.

Most of them left me empty and disappointed.

These books were like fools gold - looking like the real thing until they were tested.

It is not that these authors, who pose as experts, don't have some of the truth. Most of them, however, have no formal education and have not worked with thousands of patients, honing their skills. They are, in fact, often impostors who are copy artists, plagiarizing the views of others and pawning them off as their own, systems that are at best incomplete, failing to get their readers out of the trap of depression and other emotional ills.

As I said, there are some good books on the market as well as credible therapy systems. Most, however, are only partial and don't contain all you need to live a happy, full and purposeful live. In fact, too many offer

QUICK FIXES.

And that's it!

I am, instead, going to be taking you on a path to healing that very few discover.

CHEAP SELF-HELP BOOKS

Too often cheap, self-help books give you some of the truth, but leave out the most important parts. Many of the books that come closer are based on one of the most effective therapies for overcoming depression and other emotional problems known today. It's called Cognitive Therapy. This kind of effective therapy promotes the idea that thinking impacts feelings.

Millions of people have been helped by Cognitive Therapy.

Yet, in my analysis, these millions have not been taken far enough. They may have learned the basics and gotten some relief, but did not get TOTAL RELIEF.

Often at the heart of depression there are issues like anger, resentment, abandonment, betrayal, unresolved grief, discouragement, loss of faith and a meaninglessness that cannot be quieted. Unless these issues of the heart are addressed and aggressively attacked, the depression will never be permanently dispatched. Oh yes, it can be quieted for a time, but it will only be a temporary fix.

It is a shame that **MOST CONTEMPORARY APPROACHES TO THERAPY, INCLUDING COGNITIVE BEHAVIORAL THERAPY, FAIL TO OPEN THE DOOR TO THE HEART, PENETRATE IT, AND BRING HEALING.**

You know what I'm talking about, don't you? That's why you're reading this book.

YOU WANT MORE!

If all you do is…

…PUT ON A NEW COAT OF PAINT WHEN YOU NEED TO SCRAPE OFF THE OLD PAINT, GET RID OF THE DRY ROT AND START FRESH, YOU WILL NEVER FULLY GET OVER YOUR DEPRESSION.

My goal it to help you get free!

This is why I have three books, books that will take you to a depth where you will be transformed - TOTAL RELIEF, a totally new person!

That's what Carol needed.

It was all she could do to just get up and meet the day. After a night's sleep, the grayness of Carol's depression still hung over her like a dark cloud.

Another day. More suffering.

No hope.

Carol didn't know what to do. She wasn't just sad, a feeling that we all have at one time or other. When one is depressed, however, there is almost always a lessening of one's self-esteem where one steps into a frozen state, lasting for days, weeks, even months. This had happened with Carol, and though she had been to a therapist and taken her meds, nothing seemed to help.

She was desperate!

When I saw her, I could see the signs of depression written all over her; the sad affect, the bent frame, eyes cast downward, the short breaths, all signaling her pain. I talked with her for a moment, trying to piece together her history, and felt compassion for her condition.

She needed help.

NOW!

I had a simple, effective way to blast through her depression, a plan so effective that therapy and meds would possibly never be needed again. Carol could be whole, complete, happy, purposeful, fulfilled, flowing over with joy.

GUARANTEED!

SIMPLE, EASY TO APPLY FORMULAS THAT WORK
All it was, was just a few formulas, a few simple steps that would begin the process of taking this joyless woman and turning her into a happy, delightful, triumphant, jubilant person.

I knew it would happen.

In just a few weeks all would be changed. Carol would come into my office with a broad smile, eyes dancing, shoulders back, with a new sense of confidence.

As you read this, I can see you now…

Hoping.
Waiting.
Longing for a cure.

I want to assure you that a cure in on the way. Within a very short time…

Beginning today!

You are going to break down the bars of your prison of depression as you find the **KEY** to getting out, freeing you from those horrible feelings of depression and hopelessness.

FREE AT LAST!

TOO GOOD TO BE TRUE?

Sounds too good to be true? Well, it is good, and it is true. I have a whole system built on what is real and true, truth that I have discovered after years of searching and working with people just like you.

Of course, when you buy a book like this, you want to make sure you have a product that is not from some wacky nut who is scrapping the Milky Way with a weird approach to emotional problems.

Believe me, I have my feet firmly planted on the ground.

WHO IS DR. PAUL?
WHY CAN HE HELP?

Let me introduce myself.

I have a very diverse education, an education devoted to learning how to help people. My doctorate is from Biola University, a great university in Southern California.

For some years I studied psychology, focusing on marriage and family and wrote my doctoral dissertation on how to change one's personality. My studies at Biola University opened up to me the challenges of helping people to find happier and more fulfilling lives.

In the years that followed my education, I worked hard at developing a simple technique to do this, working with thousands of people around the world.

I recall meeting with a group of women in Ukraine, helping them to deal with their depression. There was a conference I spoke at just outside of York, England, and seminars in Romania, Russia and Bulgaria, helping people to get out of the prison of depression.

I worked with those suffering in China, Peru, France, Germany, Italy, Latvia, Moldova, Switzerland and Chili.

I did seminars in Colorado, Virginia, California, Texas, Georgia, Kentucky, Indiana, Oklahoma, Florida, New Mexico and many other places throughout the U.S., teaching, helping people to learn my special formulas - formulas that you are going to learn, formulas that will help you get over your depression…

FAST!

MY FORMULAS BRING TOTAL RELIEF

Once you learn my formulas, formulas that are fully developed in my three books, you will experience TOTAL RELIEF from your depression. Each book drills down deeper and deeper into the truth to help you understand why you are depressed and how to break free from it, once and for all.

Please start with **Book 1** to learn the basic formulas. Don't move onto Book 2 until you fully understand these principles and put them into practice. Book 1 will help many of you to begin to break free from your depression.

Then move on to **Book 2** where we will dig deeper and add to the formulas in book one. This book will plow deeper than most books on depression. It takes the formulas you learn in Book 1 and **turbo-charges** them.

Book 3 is one of those "break out" books where we uncover why you are depressed in the first place. This book will continue to add to the formulas and help you to break the underlying reasons and causes for your depression. For too long, therapists have offered only a temporary suppression of your depression. With Book 3, that will come to an end as you move toward TOTAL RELIEF. This book gets down to the heart, the spiritual and emotional core of your inner self that cries for intimacy, purpose and love.

Once you finish this book, you will be ready to live your life in a purposeful, joy-filled way that you would never have thought possible. Your inner dreams, those desires of your heart that have been shelved for too long, will come to pass.

It will be absolutely fantastic!

Years ago, when I was studying for my doctorate, I studied some of the greatest minds in the field of psychology and honed my skills as I sought to help people with their emotional problems.

LARGE PUBLISHING FIRM WANTED MY FORMULAS

Later, nearly two decades ago, I received four contracts with one of the largest publishing firms in America to produce what we were calling, "Quick Relief Kits." I was paid a handsome signing fee and worked hard to complete my kits. Then it happened: ABC News bought the company and cancelled all new contracts, including mine.

At the time, I was traveling the world and didn't have time to do anything else with the project. I kept teaching my formulas, but I never published them…

Until now!

And now you get:
- **The best**
- **The fastest**
- **A proven way…**

To heal your depression and take away the pain.

So let's get started on our journey with the goal of helping you to feel not just good again, but…

Great!
Happy!
Joyful!
Alive!

I want you to be able to blast through your depression, like Carol did and so many others around the world.

Stop now, take a deep breath, and begin a journey into joy. Help is on the way…

CHAPTER 1

BREAKTHROUGH

FORMULA 1

Folks are usually about as happy as they make up their minds to be.

Abraham Lincoln

Elizabeth's life didn't start out so well. Her dad left for another woman when she was seven, and her mom turned to drinking to overcome her sorrow. Though her mother still worked, too much of the money went for booze, and often the refrigerator was bare.

"Liz," as she was called, was not only hungry for actual food, it was the emotional hunger and nourishment that got to her the most. Many nights she would cry herself to sleep. Somehow she made it through high school and on to a community college where she met Fred, an outgoing young man who was goal driven and had lots of dreams of making it big. Within a few years they were married, and Fred graduated from college and went into a sales position with a national company. He was an instantaneous success and begin to make the big bucks. They bought a large house, Liz had a few children, and life seem absolutely fabulous…on the surface.

Below that surface, though, there seemed to be a hole in Liz's life, an ache that she didn't know how to heal. She and Fred had a good marriage, but that wasn't adequate. Liz was depressed. Fred encouraged her to see a therapist, which she did. The therapist did a lot of digging around in her past finding that her runaway father, her mother's abandonment, Liz's feelings of anger and isolation resulted in her depression.

How could it be? Liz seemed to have what any woman would want - two great kids and a loving, successful husband, yet there she was in the pits, overwhelmed by a sense of inner sadness.

Now let me say something that may shock you at first. The pain of your depression is both BAD…and GOOD. It is bad in that you FEEL the pain. No one likes to feel pain. But pain has a purpose. If your head hurts, or your knee, you go searching for a cause. The same with emotional pain. It is like an alarm system designed to alert you that something is wrong. It is a siren going off, alerting you that there is a problem that needs to be fixed. Knowing that something is wrong is GOOD.

DEPRESSION IS NOT YOUR ENEMY! Something else is, that something that is causing your depression.

So, your depression, your pain, means that there is a problem inside that needs to be fixed. We are going to discover that problem, that difficulty, that is keeping you in emotional pain. Once the problem is uncovered, you can fix it and be free from depression and its pain. In fact you can move on to TOTAL RELIEF!

I was going to do that with Liz, who had a lot of emotional pain that was robbing her of the full life she should have been experiencing.

What could I say to her to lift the depression away? Could some simple formulas work?

Yes they would!

Simple, yet so full of complexity that it will take three books to fully explain them. These simple formulas will sound familiar to you if you have read much. They are based on a therapy called, "cognitive behavioral therapy," a therapy that works with our thoughts and behavior.

I will take this kind of therapy, and as stated before, take it further than you have probably ever seen before. To do this, I will start with the basics. I did this with Liz and so many others. I have done it in seminars around the world and I will do it with you.

I have worked with people who have experienced:

1. Loss
2. Failure (moral, business)
3. Addictions that caused depression (alcohol, smoking, drugs)
4. Divorce
5. Death of a loved one
6. Chronic stress
7. Unmet needs
8. Loneliness, isolation
9. Physical reasons: birth of child, lack of sleep, aging, bad diet, thyroid or gland problems, seasonal affect disorder
10. Perfectionism
11. Anger, resentment, bitterness (at others, yourself, the world, God) and nursing it
12. Upset at the way they look, what they weigh
13. Comparisons with others
14. Hopes dashed, dreams shattered

So many things can cause depression. But no matter what the cause, these formulas of mine work.

It doesn't matter what you are feeling or what happened to you or is happening right now, my formulas will help you to climb out of the "pits" and bring you to a place where you can enjoy your life, once again, maybe for the first time.

Don't look at my formulas, think you understand them already, close the book and go looking for answers somewhere else. That would be a big mistake. Why? We are talking about TOTAL RELIEF in this series on depression. To arrive at the place of total relief you need to take some simple steps, steps that will be easy to understand and comprehend.

MAKE A COMMITMENT

So why don't you, right now, make a commitment to yourself to finish my system of TOTAL RELIEF? Study the formulas I give. Take your time to understand them and put them into practice. To help you learn my formulas, I have developed special workbooks for each book called: **Ten Days To A New Life** along with with Dr. Paul's **Quick Relief YES! Cards**, cards that will help in the process of TOTAL RELIEF. You will be able to download the YES! Cards to your kindle, I-Pad, I-Phone or other android device and speed up the process. Or you can order any of my books, workbooks or cards in print from amazon.com.

SOUL MEDICATION THAT WORKS

Now what you are reading is not just a book of information. **I want you to see me here working with you. You are in my office and Dr. Paul is going to help.** I care deeply about you and your pain. I have the soul medication that is going to help. You, however, need to take the medication.

Make the decision now. Say, "YES! I will learn these formulas and work hard to apply them to my life."

Of course you are going to have doubts. You have tried to get rid of your depression so many times before. "Will Dr. Paul's system work," you ask? "Is it what you have been longing for?"

YES it is! The doctor is here to help.

Now on to the formula, the breakthrough... FORMULA 1.

This formula is so simple that it will at first catch you by surprise. It is…

T + A = F

I want you to look at this formula for a moment.

Pause.

Say it to yourself. Oh yes, there is no breakthrough yet. But I want you to look at it and to know that this formula is going to bring you help, maybe even today.

What does the formula mean?

Thoughts + Actions = Feelings

Simple, isn't it? T + A = F. But effective! Wait until you fully understand this formula and how to practice it in your life. It is going to free you from your depression.

Some of you may think that you understand the formula and how it works. But believe me, you don't. There is a lot more to this formula that I will help you understand. It goes deep. And that's where the healing comes from - understanding its depth.

THREE UNIQUE FORMULAS IN THIS BOOK

Once I get done explaining my three formulas in this book, you will never be the same again. To break out of your prison, you must stay with me and learn the KEY to opening the door of your depression and getting out…

Finally.

For good!

You see, **YOUR FEELINGS ARE HELD HOSTAGE BY WHAT YOU THINK AND WHAT YOU DO.**

See the word, "hostage"?

Your wrong thinking and actions have put you in an emotional prison where you can't get out. You are stuck behind the bars and can't find the key. That's why you feel desperate! What's the key that will unlock the door of your depression?

Let me write this statement again and notice the words I emphasize.

Your *FEELINGS* Are Held *HOSTAGE* By What You *THINK* And What You *DO*.

Throughout my books I am going to talk about three important essentials:
1. **Thoughts**
2. **Actions**
3. **You**

We will see how all three need to be understood to get you out of your prison of depression.

STAY WITH ME IF YOU WANT TO BE FREE

I am laying the building blocks that will in time be absolutely magical. You are going to be free!

———————————————

SUMMARY: Change your thoughts and actions and you will change your feelings…for the good!

CHAPTER 2

The KEY that Unlocks The Door To Depression

THOUGHTS

Remember, happiness doesn't depend upon who you are or what you have, it depends solely upon what you think.

        Dale Carnegie

John was not one to admit to any pain. He had been a high school star in basketball, gone to college and made a name for himself. Then John went on to business, becoming a successful CPA overseeing a large office and becoming an important part of his community.

But John often suffered from depression, so severe at times that he finally sought help.

It's hard for many men to acknowledge their pain. That macho part of the male ego often is unable to admit that they have a problem that they can't solve.

John came to my office and bared his soul. "Can you help me?" he said with a sense of desperation.

After getting John's history, I gave him *formula 1*, $T + A = F$, a formula you have seen, but do not know yet how it works. I shared with John that his feelings were held hostage by what he was thinking and doing.

At first he did not understand. He said that he had tried the "power of positive thinking," and that did not work. I smiled when he said that, because the power of positive thinking often does not work.

Turning to him I said confidently, "I am going to help you to think in a way you have never thought before, not just paint some positive thoughts over your depression. That rarely works. After a few sessions, you will know how to use this formula. We will drill down to a depth that you have never thought possible."

John gave me a smile and nodded, showing me that he understood. As I looked at him, I saw eyes that were empty, as if there was nothing there, yet I knew that if he kept coming, those eyes would be dancing with joy.

FORMULA 1

Now, when we look at *formula* 1, T + A + F, (Thoughts + Actions = Feelings) we must first look at what we are thinking.

I must say at this point that it is going to take three books to fully understand just this one word, "thoughts," how they work and how to radically change them so that you can be liberated from your depression. If you stay with me all the way, you are going to make a fantastic breakthrough.

But first I must start on the ground floor.

When we change our thoughts we will change how we feel. And it can happen fast. A person can move from depression to happiness in seconds.

That's basic to formula 1.

Let me illustrate.

HOW FAST FORMULA 1 CAN WORK

Teresa is depressed. She has a husband who is a sports nut. During the football season he is glued to the TV watching not only the pro teams, but many of the college games too. He only grunts when she tells him that food is on the table, rarely carrying on a conversation with her.

You can see why Teresa is depressed. She feels neglected, unappreciated, even unnecessary. Those thoughts have imprisoned her. How could they ever be changed? You see, if you change your thoughts, you will change how you feel. It's that simple. But how could Teresa's thoughts change in light of her situation?

Today the Super Bowl is on, and there sits Teresa's husband in his normal position, focused on the TV, with a beer by his side. He is happy. But Teresa is not. She sits in the other room, still in her bathrobe and slippers, wishing she was dead.

Then the doorbell rings. "Hank! There's someone at the door," Teresa screams out in an irritated voice.

But Hank is too focused to hear.

Angry that he is ignoring her once again, Teresa eases herself out of the couch, and, in a slumped over posture, moves to the door and opens it.

Surprise! It is the magazine sweepstakes team awarding her 10 million dollars! There are balloons, trumpets blasting and a small celebration taking place right in front of her door.

Teresa, though depressed as she walked up to the door, is a changed person. She is now dancing, laughing, clapping her hands and full of cheer. Happiness and joy have shoved out her depression…

In an instant!

Even Hank, seeing the commotion, stops watching football and gets in on the action. He and Teresa are hugging, kissing, and exploding with joy. Wow! Life couldn't get any better than this.

Now let's analyze what happened with Teresa. Let's apply *formula 1*.

Teresa, first of all, had been thinking how neglected and unappreciated she was. Those thoughts resulted in depression. Then came the 10 million dollars and knowing that she and Hank were rich. They could take those trips they had dreamed of, be together, be a family again.

Joy exploded in her mind as these **new thoughts** shoved out the old ones. And it all happened in less than a minute. It was like a 60 Second Cure.

Bam!

Now, I don't want you to think that your depression is going to be cured in 60 seconds. It would be nice, but, unless someone shows up at your door with 10 million dollars, you need more time to understand my formulas and how to apply them.

To be honest, Teresa's depression could very well come back after the shock of being given all that money wore off. Getting rich is not the answer to depression. In fact, many wealthy individuals are very depressed. Why? They seem to have it all, all but one thing; they have never learned the true formulas that turn depression into happiness, formulas you are learning right now.

All you have to know now is this: When thoughts are changed, feelings will be changed. In other words,

YOUR THOUGHTS RIGHT NOW ARE MAKING YOU DEPRESSED.

I know that statement hits you in the face, and you are going to deny it. You believe that it's your CIRCUMSTANCES that are making you depressed, don't you? If you could only get a new husband, or if your kids would treat you right, or if your mother would quick nagging you, or if you hadn't messed up so much, or if you only had more money, and on and on.

But you are mistaken.

DON'T QUIT READING UNTIL YOU UNDERSTAND MY FORMULAS

Now don't close the book and feel sorry that I don't understand you. I know what you are thinking and feeling. You have to stay with me so that I can prove to you what is really making you depressed. After all, I have helped thousands break loose from the chains of depression and other emotional difficulties.

I want to break you free from your prison. I have the key!

In a few chapters I will show you why it's not your circumstances that are causing your pain. It's your THOUGHTS.

Period.

Now, I realize that thoughts are hard to change. The groove you have made over a number of years in your brain are thoughts that have made a deep channel in your mind.

I AM GOING TO HELP YOU CHANGE YOUR THOUGHTS!

I know that thoughts are often automatic and difficult to change, but you are going to learn how to change those thoughts. I'm going to give you some keys, further formulas that will break you out of your prison, make new grooves in your brain, and free you from your depression, once and for all.

So it's your thoughts that are keeping you chained. How can you change them? Soon you are going to find out. Let's keep looking at FORMULA 1.

John, Liz and Carol stayed with me. They trusted me to help. And I didn't let them down.

SUMMARY: The easiest way to feel great is to change your thoughts.

CHAPTER 3

Another KEY That Helps To Get You Out Of Depression

ACTION

> *I never worry about action, but only inaction.*
>
> Winston Churchill

Thoughts can be so ingrained in our minds that it is often hard to break loose from them. Suzzie sure did. It was early on in my work that I discovered that cognitive therapy, working solely on thoughts alone fell short for some people. I had to do something else.

In my doctoral studies, decades ago, I read a story by either Ann Landers or Dear Abby that captured my attention. I'm not sure which one recounted the story, and I may not remember it exactly as it was written, but in the story had a nugget of truth that changed the way I practiced my therapy. I not only focused on thinking but also on actions. That's why FORMULA 1 does not just talk about thoughts. Look at the formula:

T + A = F.

You see that feelings are held hostage by what we THINK and what we DO. Both are important to understand.

Let me share with you the story I read by one of those newspaper columnists years ago. This will help you understand the formula and how ACTIONS are important in getting over your depression.

A woman came to her attorney depressed and angry. She asked him to help her divorce her husband. "Beyond just getting a divorce, I want to hurt him as much as possible," she proclaimed.

The attorney, a wise man, delved further into her story. She had been married for over 30 years to a very successful man - big home, the finest cars, best vacations, all that one could wish for. But a rift had occurred in their relationship. Differences of opinions, and busy-ness had robbed them of their time together, with the result that they moved to separate bedrooms and lived separate lives.

This woman grew to hate her husband because of his neglect of her and her needs. Depression had set in, and she finally had to do something about it…get even.

"So you want to hurt him?" questioned the attorney.
"Very much," answered the woman.

"Tell me this," the attorney asked. "Will your husband be glad that you want a divorce?"

"I'm sure he hates me as much as I hate him," came the answer. "He will be glad to rid his life of me."

"Then a divorce alone, the dividing of the property will not hurt him."

The attorney then turned, looked at the woman with a smile on his face. "I know how to hurt your husband. Call him up and have lunch together. Tell him that you have acted badly and want to restore the relationship. Declare to him your love and ask if you can move back into the bedroom."

"I could never do that. It's a lie," proclaimed the woman, "and I don't feel I could ever do such a thing."

"Yes, it's a lie. But if he is sucked into it and allows you back into his life believing that you really love him, you have a great possibility of hurting him, really hurting him. Do it for 30 days and then come back. You will cause great pain."

So the woman took a chance. She hated this man so much that she was willing to put on this ruse, to trap him, deceive him and then jerk him by getting the divorce.

The lunch worked as she affirmed her love. She moved back into the bedroom with him, did all the things a loving wife would do, ate with him, wrote him notes affirming her love, praised him for his fine qualities, smiled once again, kissed him and made love.

It was quite the 30 day ruse, and he fell for it, fell hard. Within a few weeks he was buying her jewelry. They even spent a weekend in one of their favorite resorts. He was calling her from his office, breaking away to have lunch together and sharing times of intimacy that they had not shared together for years.

What a fabulous plan the attorney had given her. This husband didn't know what was going to hit him. Soon he would be emotionally bleeding, stripped bare from the one he had fallen in love with again.

After 30 days this woman came back to her attorney's office. When she sat down in his office, she looked at him with a new energy and vibrancy. "I have come to say that I am not going to divorce my husband."

"You are not going to divorce your husband?" the attorney said with surprise! "I thought you hated him, that you wanted to hurt him."

"I did. But things have changed," she exclaimed with a bold smile. "I have discovered, through this ruse we planned, through acting it out, that my husband is the greatest man alive."

Quite a story, isn't it? And, from what I remember it is true. This really happened.

"So, what does it have to do with depression?" you ask.

It's that part of FORMULA 1.

T + **A** = F.

Thoughts + **ACTIONS** = Feelings.

Actions can have a powerful impact on your feelings as demonstrated in the last story, or as they often put it: "You can ACT yourself to a new way of feeling."

Did you get that?

YOU CAN **ACT** YOURSELF TO A NEW WAY OF FEELING.

I have found in my therapy with others and in the many seminars I have done around the world, that for some, it is almost impossible to change their thoughts. The thoughts are so ingrained that the person finds it difficult to do cognitive therapy alone. They need cognitive-BEHAVIORAL therapy. So, I start with the action side of the formula first.

At seminars I have often had people turn to each other, people who may be depressed, and say with a big smile on their face, "I feel so depressed." Then everybody laughs. It is hard to feel depressed with a big smile on your face.

Try it now. Come on, I can see you! Put a big smile on your face. Experiment. See what it does for you. Try to hold the smile for the next 3 minutes. You will almost certainly feel better. There is something magic about acting and how it changes how we feel.

Now I know what you're thinking (there's that word, thinking). Your thoughts are already attacking this whole idea of acting. You think: "I don't want to be a phony." And that's a good thought. I am not asking you to be a phony, to lie to yourself, to distort reality. What I am asking you to do is to take some simple steps that will get you over your depression.

For example, depressed people normally have shallow breaths. As a result, reduced oxygen goes to the brain, clouding the thought process and making the person feel more depressed. Change your breathing (an action) and you can change how you feel.

The ACT of even sitting up straight so that you can take a deep breath can produce feelings that will counteract your depression.

Now let me ask you a question: Are you being a phony by practicing deep breathing instead of continuing the process of shallow breaths? Of course not! You realize that you can actually change how you feel by this action step; change your breathing.

So, if I ask you to walk around with a smile on your face, am I asking you to be a phony? No! Depressed people usually walk around with a sad look, a sad affect, even a frown. When I ask you to change that affect and put on a smile or even laugh, it is no different than asking you to breathe deeply. You are not being a phony. You are correcting a problem from another source, not by changing your thoughts but by changing your actions.

It's that simple.

Yet powerful!

Years ago, Norman Cousins laughed himself to health, and laugh therapy, at least in its popular form, was born. According to some studies, laugh therapy provides a number of benefits of which some apply directly to one who is depressed.

1. Enhances oxygen intake (because a depressed person often does not take deep breaths)

2. Relaxes muscles throughout the body

3. Relieves pain

4. Improves mental functions like alertness, memory and creativity

5. **Improves Overall Attitude** (and that's what you want, isn't it?)

6. Reduces stress and tension

7. Triggers the **Release Of Endorphins That Kill Both Natural And Emotional Pain**

8. Promotes relaxation

9. Improves sleep

10. PRODUCES A **GENERAL SENSE OF WELL-BEING**

Look at the value of laughter. What benefits it has for a depressed person!

"But," you say, "I don't feel like laughing. I'm depressed, you know."

Of course, I know that you are depressed. That's why you are reading my TOTAL RELIEF program to release you from the prison of depression. One of the ways to do this is to change your thoughts. We will develop that much more in the next chapter and the next few books. For now, however, you need to also work on the other side by changing your actions.

Of course you don't feel like it. You are depressed! And you can stay there if you like. You can live a very unhappy and unproductive life if you CHOOSE. And that's it - CHOICE.

You can CHOOSE to break out of your depression. It's not going to be easy. The habits you have developed that keep you in this prison are deeply ingrained. It is going to take some work, some effort. But YOU CAN DO IT! I know you can. I have seen thousands use my formulas to break loose and have happy and productive lives.

So try it. Breathe. Smile. Laugh. It will make all the difference.

Oh yes, you will not feel TOTAL RELIEF, at least not yet. But you will begin the journey of understanding why you are depressed and begin to break out of your prison one bar at a time.

Nearly 30 years ago, I woke up in the dumps - depressed and defeated. A meeting the night before had sent me spiraling downward. How could I break out?

So I tried laugh therapy. On my way to the office I began to laugh out loud as I drove my car. I really got with it as I moved up to a stop light, laughing as hard as I could. Without realizing it, another car moved up beside me as I was lost in my laughter. Soon I realized that the other driver was staring at me, wondering, I'm sure, whether I had lost it or not!

Well, I had lost it, my depression. That short session in the car worked. Laughter was the medicine I needed.

What I am seeking to do in this chapter is to show you that certain action steps can help you overcome your depression. There are many other forms of action that you can do to attack your depression and gain victory over it. More about this later.

At this juncture, I wanted only to introduce to you the formula with some illustrations of how it works. The woman who moved from despising her husband to loving him, the changes that happen from deep breathing, smiling and laughter, all illustrate how ACTION is one of the key parts to my special formula in conquering depression.

$T + A = F$

Thoughts + Action = Feelings.

Your FEELINGS are held hostage by what you THINK and what you DO. That's it. It's a simple, basic formula this is going to help you break loose from your depression.

But you need further understanding. I will continue in this book and then dig a lot deeper in Book 2. You're going to like it.

So hold on and keep reading. There's some good stuff to come!
_____-

SUMMARY: When thinking is not working for you, actions are the secret to unleashing new feelings that will change your life.

CHAPTER 4

BREAKTHROUGH

FORMULA 2

What upsets people is not things themselves but their judgments about things.

Epictetus A.D. 50-130

When Mary sat down with me she told me a story full of tragedy. No wonder she was depressed! Her high school aged daughter was killed in a car accident after her daughter's drunk boyfriend ran the car into a tree. Then, Mary got breast cancer, and to add injury to injury, her husband decided to leave her for another woman after 23 years of marriage. All of this in a period of three years, all of it crashing down on her, suffocating her, strangling any joy she had.

I FEEL THE PAIN OF OTHERS, YOUR PAIN

As I sat with Mary, I could feel her pain. "How can I help her?" I said to myself. For a moment, I was stuck in her pain and felt its tentacles around my emotional throat.

I hope you understand that even though I have a doctorate in my field of study, even though I have all my formulas that help people break loose from many emotional ills: depression, anxiety, fear, loneliness, anger, stress and many other prisons that people are in, I too feel these same feelings.

There are times I am swamped by my feelings. Oh yes, I ultimately know what to do. But I have to work at it like anyone else. I have to take my formulas and put them into practice.

So there I was, feeling Mary's pain.

I could tell her about thoughts and actions and breaking out of her depression. But that would be cruel at this time. "Breathe Mary, breath. Laugh. Smile. Think positively." No, I couldn't start with that, not at this time of her deep sharing.

I do believe that depression is almost always self-defeating. Mary could hold on to it, but it is never virtuous to feel wretched, emotionally defeated and to wallow in self-pity. To be human in the way we were meant to be, is to learn how to crawl out of our dark prisons, to climb above the difficulties and to find peace and joy no matter what the circumstances.

I HAVE EXPERIENCED A LOT OF PAIN

Now this is what I firmly believe and practice in my own life. I have lost a wife to cancer after 43 years of marriage. I have experienced all kinds of setbacks and difficulties, yet I find in every case these formulas I am teaching you not only help, but give me hope. I can choose to take the worst life throws at me and still come out with a smile!

But, I couldn't throw this belief and practice of mine at Mary, hitting her straight on. I would have to go slowly, show that I cared, and then introduce my formulas.

What did I do?

I told her that it was all right for her to be depressed. I took her by the hand and prayed:

Dear God,
So much has gone on in Mary's life, so much pain, pain piled upon pain. It's incomprehensible. Yet here we are trying to figure a way out. Help me to help Mary through this pain, this torment, so that she may, someday, find peace and joy again.
Amen.

Oh, I haven't told you that along with a doctorate in psychology I also have a masters in theology. I do believe in God and pray a lot. But in this first book I am not going to go into a lot of "God-stuff". There are too many who say, "Just pray about it," and leave it at that.

Before we get into beliefs and how they impact our thinking, I want to make sure you understand my basic formulas first. We will cover BELIEFS in Book 2, a powerful study that gets to the core of what is making so many depressed.

Now back to Mary.

What I did with Mary, I want to do with you. You have your own story about what is causing your pain. I don't want to take your pain lightly. There is a lot of hurt that is producing your depression. There are good reasons for it. I know. I have worked with so many, looking into their eyes, hearing their stories, feeling their pain.

I had to ultimately help Mary through her pain. If I were a medical doctor and you came into my office with horrible back pain, I wouldn't just stand there and empathize with you. No! I would prescribe you a type of pain medication that would get you through your agony and then, later, seek to get at the root problem.

In one sense this is what I am doing with you.

Book 1 is helping you with the PAIN.

And this is what I was going to do with Mary. She was being tormented by past hurts, and losses that continued to impact her.

I said something like this. "Mary, I'm going to give you a prescription to help you overcome your pain. Like any prescription, it will take time for it to begin working. You are going to feel this sense of hopelessness and depression for a little while longer. That's OK, but there's hope. If you do what I ask you to do, you will break out of this prison you are in, finally, for good."

So I began the process that lasted for eight sessions, helping Mary to understand my formulas, these prescriptions for a toxic soul.

First we had to deal with her thoughts, all the grief about her daughters death, her breast cancer and a husband who walked out of her. There was a lot of anger, and rightfully so, as well as unforgiveness, bitterness and resentment all swirling around in this pot that brewed up the depression she had.

A SMILE RETURNED TO HER FACE

To help her understand more fully how thoughts lead to feelings, I introduced her to my second formula, FORMULA 2. Once she understood how this formula worked, she was on her way to healing.

Now it didn't happen overnight, but it did happen within the eight weeks we were working together. A smile returned to her sad face, a new bounce in her step, and joy began to replace her hopelessness.

Oh, my formulas didn't change the tragedies that happened to her. Instead, they gave her a way to see life in a new way, a way that opened the door to the prison of depression, freed her and set her on a pathway to a new life.

What is FORMULA 2?

Let me give you a formula that most people instinctively believe, $E = F$ or…

Events = Emotions

What the formula states is that the things that happen to us, these triggering events, are the situations that produce our emotions. In Mary's case, the death of her daughter, the breast cancer and her husband leaving her were all responsible for producing her emotional state, her feelings, and thus her depression.

That makes sense doesn't it?

We blame the events that are happening, the situations that occur, the circumstances. We sincerely believe that if we could change the circumstances, we could change our feelings.

If only…then I would be happy.

If only I had another…
Husband
Wife
Kids
Mother
Father
Friend

Body

Chance

House

If only I had more…

Money

Friends

Time

Happiness

Fun

If only I could…

Start fresh again

Be myself

Find myself

Find a purpose for my life

Forget the past

Find my soul mate

Be content and at peace

IF ONLY

Oh, we could add so many more. But you get the point. We all tend to believe that events are responsible for our emotional state. If we could only change what is happening around us, we would finally be happy. So, we dream of changing what is happening on the outside and never realize that it is what is going on INSIDE OF US that needs to be changed.

What do I mean?

You see, the Events = Emotions formula is misleading. Believing it will get you into trouble. That's why you are depressed right now. You believe that some event, some happening, has caused your depression.

A triggering event (a happening, a situation) has produced your feelings of depression (this emotion or feeling), or:

E = E.

Though this formula makes sense, you have been lied to.

In the beginning of this book, I told a story about a wife who was sitting on the couch, a football widow. If you recall, she was gripped with depression. When the door bell rang, and there stood the magazine sweepstakes people awarding her 10 million dollars, her depression stopped instantly. Why? Was it the event? "Yes," you say. "If that happened to me, my depression would leave instantaneously."

You see, we all believe that if good things happen to us we will be happy. But if bad things happen we will be sad, even depressed. It all makes sense.

Mary had some very bad things happen to her. Maybe if she could find a new and loving husband all would be well again.

Only if…thinking. And it is this kind of thinking that gets us into trouble. It is built on a false premise, a false formula for happiness, Events = Emotion.

Then what is the right formula, FORMULA 2?

This formula is going to change your life. So hold on. Buckle your seat belt and get ready for the ride of your life!

FORMULA 2, is written this way:

E + I = E, or...

EVENTS + INTERPRETATION = EMOTION

Every event is interpreted by us. It is NOT the event that causes the emotion but our INTERPRETATION of that event. Mary's depression was caused by her interpretation of what had happened to her.

AREN'T I BEING A LITTLE HARSH?

Now this may seem harsh to you at first, but stay with me. I am not saying that Mary should not feel the pain and loss of a child, her breasts, and rejection by her former husband. To feel the emotional pain is healthy. But when it hangs on and on and on and there is no recovery, we have to look deeper at what is causing this emotional pain.

As we look deeper, we will discover the key. Mary's interpretation of those events that happened to her, events that she blames for her depression are in reality what IS MAKING HER DEPRESSED.

MARY IS ACTUALLY MAKING HERSELF DEPRESSED!

It is important that you understand this. **Don't shut the book and think I'm being insensitive, that I don't care, that I don't take what happened to Mary or to you as being significant.**

As I said earlier, I was heartsick when I listened to Mary's story. But what was I to do, leave her in her pain? Were the tragic circumstances that happened to her going to, from now on, define her life? Was her life to be lived in continual pain and depression without a cure?

No! Never!

Mary's life could have a new beginning, and so can yours!

We see that FORMULA 2 shows us that it is our interpretations of the events that happen to us that get us depressed. That's it.

Now it will take a lot more understanding to learn how to give the events that have made you depressed, a new interpretation. In fact, in Book 2, I will give you other formulas that will build on FORMULA 2, formulas that will take you to a new depth of understanding.

Don't go there now, though, before I am able to lay the proper foundation. You must understand the three formulas I give in this book and practice using them. Then you will be ready for Book 2.

As I sat with Mary, I covered FORMULA 1, how our feelings are held hostage by what we think and do, or THOUGHTS + ACTIONS = FEELINGS. The loss of her daughter, breasts, and husband was her focus when she came to my office. She was hunched over, a sad affect on her face, with pain written all over her in bold letters.

Then I covered Formula 2, Events + Interpretations = Emotions. As we focused on this formula, I asked:

"What are you thinking about your daughter?"

Mary burst out: "I will never see her graduate from high school and college. She was such a beautiful girl with a contagious personality. I will never be able to see her get married, have children and allow me to be a grandmother. Why did it have to happen? Where was God?"

"I have no answers," she said, "just an inner pain that will not go away."

Mary's thoughts were making her depressed. How could she change them and still live in the reality of her loss?

WHAT THOUGHTS REALLY ARE

You see, thoughts are made up of INTERPRETATIONS. That's what thoughts really are. We all are interpreting all the time. Right now, as you read what I am saying, you are making conclusions, interpreting. You can't help it. That's the way the mind works, processing, evaluating, interpreting.

So it is not the event that causes your emotional pain, but your interpretation of the event.

Mary was interpreting her events as evil, and that interpretation made her feel bad. Could her interpretations be changed so she could feel good, even happy?

Yes!

How? How can you take such horrific events that happened to her and come out feeling good?

We do it by a process called "flipping." Think of a coin, heads and tails. You have heard the expression, "Heads you win, tails you lose." You flip your interpretation from the tails side where you are losing to the heads side where you win. This kind of flipping, switching or reframing, if understood, will help you move out of your depression.

As I talked with Mary about the tragic loss of her daughter, I asked her if there was any way to look at the same event and come out with feelings of joy? When I said this, she looked at me puzzled. "How can I do this? It's all tragic," she exclaimed.

"True, it is without question, tragic. But there can be other interpretations of your daughter than the ones you have."

"How?" Mary asked.

I took all of Mary's interpretations of the event and began to show her a way to re-interpret her daughter's life. Up to this point, she had focused on the horrible accident, the loss, the memories that she would never have: graduation, marriage, grandkids.

"If all you do is focus on her tragic loss, you will never break loose from your depression," I said, with understanding.

So I taught Mary how to "flip" her interpretation to one that was true, not something phony, but an interpretation that she could embrace.

"I can tell you loved your daughter so much. Tell me about her."

Mary began to tell me about her vibrant personality, how much fun she was. "She had such a joyous approach to life, full of laughter and pleasure. I don't know of a girl that had such a peaceful approach to life and the gifts she had! She was the star on the girls soccer team, sang the lead part in a school play, had gobs of friends, and was voted president of her class."

"What a girl!"

As she talked, I could see Mary's eyes begin to sparkle. For a moment her daughter was alive, walking through the many great memories she had.

"Mary," I said. "You just flipped your interpretation."

"I did?"

"Yes. As you recalled all the great things about your daughter, I could see your mood change. A smile splashed across you face for the first time since I've known you. It was magic."

FLIPPING...THE KEY TO BREAKING OUT OF DEPRESSION

Mary and I talked for a while about flipping and how to do it, not only with her daughter, but with the breast cancer and her husband's running off with another woman.

As I said before, within eight weeks, she learned how to change her interpretations, always in line with the truth, to bring about good feelings.

A few years ago, I was calling on some women in my area for our church. One woman, in her 80's told me about her husband and their 60 plus years of marriage. A few years before, he had died, and she had fixated on his death. "Why would God ever take my husband away from me?" she asked.

Later on in the day, I visited another woman about the same age. Her husband of over 60 years had been dead for only a few months, yet she exclaimed to me: "I thank God everyday for the 60 plus years he gave me to live with my husband."

What a difference between these two women. The same event. But a different emotion. Why?

FLIPPING or reframing.

One took the event and only saw the bad. The other saw the same event and focused on the good. One was depressed. The other joyous.

You see, you need to PUT YOUR INTERPRETATIONS ON TRIAL. Look at them. Test them. They are either making you sick or bringing life and joy. (Much more on this in Book 2 - how to put your interpretations on trial.)

That's the secret to FORMULA 2, a secret that will blast away your depression and break you free from your prison into a world of beauty and joy.

EVENTS + INTERPRETATION = EMOTION

Change your interpretation and you will change your emotion… guaranteed!

Remember the depressed woman who won the 10 million dollars? At first there was great joy! "I'm rich!" And she could see what all the money could do for her and her husband.

But then it dawned on her: If she took the cash option and paid the taxes, she would lose over half of it. She would only get 4.8 million dollars. "What a shame," she uttered under her breath. That made her mad, and soon she was back in her depression.

You see, you can actually take a good event, interpret it in such a way that will make you feel sad. Or you can reverse it, take a bad, even a horrible situation like Mary's, or yours, reinterpret it and come out feeling good.

It's all up to you.

To help you understand more fully how "flipping" works, let me take a lot of events, happenings, situations that you or anyone might face. I might not take your situation, but this will help you understand how to flip or reframe an interpretation that is making you feel bad to one that makes you feel good.

NOT THE POWER OF POSITIVE THINKING ALONE

Now I hope you understand that I am NOT talking about the power of positive thinking. At times there might be some value in this, but often these thoughts are not in line with reality.

A man, who was trying to think positively, came to my office one day. He kept saying to himself that one day he would be wealthy, all the while sitting on the couch, not doing a thing! This kind of talking does nothing. It is not in touch with reality. I would rather you practice the *power of reality thinking,* thinking thoughts that are true and honest. It is this kind of thinking that ultimately wins and brings you out of your dismal prison of depression.

What I want you to see is that new interpretations you come up with, flipping from one that is getting you depressed to one that will bring joy into your life, will be based on truth, on reality. No made up fiction. No lying to yourself. That won't work.

So let me list a number of situations, events where I will add an interpretation that will get you depressed, then flip it and add some that will switch off the kind of emotions that lead to depression, flipping them to a more positive, truthful outlook.

Here goes, learning how to manage, FLIP, switch, and reframe our interpretations.

EVENT	INTERPRETATIONS FLIP IT, REFRAMING	EMOTION
Cancer	Why is this happening to me?	Depression
	How can I go on?	Hopelessness
	I might die.	Grief
	God must hate me.	Disappointment
	I am going to learn from this experience.	Peace
	Thank God for the many people who are going to help me. I'm so lucky!	Joy. Gratitude
	If I die I'd go to heaven.	Hope
Lost my job	We are going to go broke and lose our home.	Depression
	This is unfair.	Anger
	I am going to work hard and find another job	Encouragement
	I am thankful for the job I did have.	Gratitude
My husband left	How could he do this to me?	Depression

EVENT	INTERPRETA-TIONS FLIP IT, REFRAMING	EMOTION
	I've wasted my life on that jerk!	Anger
	I won't have enough money.	Hopelessness
	I will figure a way out of this.	Hope
	Thank God I have friends to support me.	Joy
	I will focus on things I have and not on the husband I lost.	Encouragement
Investment down	I won't be able to retire.	Hopelessness
	Who is going to take care of me?	Confusion
	I give up.	Depression
	Stocks will come back. They always do.	Hope.
	Delayed retirement doesn't mean I can't enjoy my life.	Encouragement

EVENT	INTERPRETA-TIONS FLIP IT, REFRAMING	EMOTION
Problem Children	Why did I ever have kids?	Anger
	I feel so rejected.	Depression
	They don't treat me right.	Resentment
	No matter what they do, I will show my love to them.	Determination
	Even though they are not behaving the right way, I choose to love them and thank God for them.	Joy Peace
Health Problems	I'm sick of being sick!	Depression
	Why me?	Hopelessness
	I feel miserable all the time.	Resentment
	Why does God let bad things happen to good people? This sucks!	Doubt
	At least I'm alive!	Hope

	I will not let my sickness define who I am.	Determination
	I will focus on the many other good things I have and not my sickness.	Joy Gratitude
	What can I learn from my sickness?	Anticipation
People Problems	Why do they act like jerks?	Anger
	I will never talk with them again.	Resentment Bitterness
	I have no true friends.	Depression
	I will continue to be a friend.	Determination
	Though others may reject me, I accept myself and know that I am a good person.	Hope
	I will find a good friend if I keep being a loving, friendly person.	Happiness
Father is a jerk.	Why did I get such a jerk of a father?	Depression

	When will he ever learn to treat me right?	Misery
	My dad's a jerk, but I still love him.	Hope
	I will always show outward love to my father through my actions and words.	Determination
	Though my dad acts like a jerk at times, I choose to thank God for my dad.	Joy Gratitude
A flat tire	Why now?	Anger
	This always happens to me!	Depression Hopelessness
	I have a spare tire.	Joy
	"Flats happen."	Peace
Work Problems	I hate this job!	Anger Frustration Disgust
	I'll never get ahead.	Depression
	It's 12 years before I can retire.	Hopelessness
	The pay is miserable.	Discouragement
	At least I have a job!	Gratefulness

EVENT	INTERPRETATIONS FLIP IT, REFRAMING	EMOTION
	If I am patient, I can find a better job.	Hope
	Though I have a sad job, I choose to be happy.	Joy
	The pain I feel is going to make me a better person.	Peace
My husband died	I can't make it.	Hopelessness
	I wish I were dead.	Depression
	I hurt so much.	Grief
	"God. Why did you let this happen?"	Anger
	Thank you God for letting us live this long together.	Gratitude
	I will miss him terribly, but I will make it and find joy again.	Hope
	He's in heaven and having a great time.	Joy
I have no real friends	I'm worthless.	Depression

	No one likes me.	Worthlessness
	Nothing will ever change.	Hopelessness
	Until I find a friend, I will be a friend to myself.	Peace
	I will go to church and join a group.	Hope
	I will stop moping and start coping!	Determination
	I will make someone a great friend!	Confidence Joy
I have no energy to do anything	I'm worn out trying to help.	Hopelessness
EVENT	**INTERPRETA-TIONS FLIP IT, REFRAMING**	**EMOTION**
	This overwhelms me.	Helplessness
	Sleeping is my best option.	Lethargy/failure
	Whatever I do will be wrong.	Guilt
	I don't feel like it, but I'm going to tackle the problem.	Determination

	I choose to be energetic.	Hope
	When I smile, I feel energetic!	Joy
I have too many things to do.	I will never get done.	Frustration
	I never get to enjoy my life.	Hopelessness
	Why doesn't somebody help?	Anger
	I will do at least one thing.	Determination
	If I do just one thing a day, I will get the job done by the weekend.	Hope
	Having something to do gives me purpose.	Joy
I can't sleep	Something is wrong with me.	Sadness
	Why do other people sleep so well?	Jealousy
	Life sucks!	Anger
	I am going to talk with my doctor. He might be able to help.	Hope

EVENT	INTERPRETATIONS FLIP IT, REFRAMING	EMOTION
	I accept the way I am.	Peace
	I will sign up for a relaxation course.	Determination
Impossible situations	It's out of control!	Hopelessness
	I give up.	Failure
	Is it "I can't" or "I won't"?	Reflective
	I will!	Determination
	I did it!	Joy
Bad decisions	Nothing turns out the way it should.	Hopelessness
	Bad people are too often in control.	Frustration
	I'm going to tell him off.	Anger
	Life is not fair, but I will still be fair.	Determination
	I will always stand up for what is right.	Purpose

	My happiness is not determined by what happens outside of my control.	Joy
My husband lied to me	What a schmuck!	Anger
	I will never trust him again.	Distrust
	All men are liars.	Resentment
	Yes, he lied, but I still love him.	Hope
	Liars often fear telling the truth. I will make it safe for him to tell the truth.	Determination
	I will forgive him.	Peace
The waitress is ignoring me	Who does she think she is?	Disgust
	When will she ever wait on me?	Impatience
	What a klutz!	Anger
	No one ever pays attention to me.	Depression
	Wow! She is really busy.	Understanding
	Relax. I have nothing else to do.	Peace

	What beautiful eyes she has!	Joy
Why is he frowning at me?	People who frown are angry.	Perplexed
	Everyone should smile at me.	Disappointment
	Frowns mean I'm a failure.	Failure
	I will greet his frown with a smile.	Determination
	His frown has nothing to do with me.	Peace
	I am going to try to get him to smile.	Joy
Look how much I weigh!	I'm a failure.	Failure
	To be liked, I must be thin.	Hopelessness
	Fat is ugly.	Depression
	Fat is beautiful!	Joy
	I choose to be happy though fat!	Glad
	My joy is not dependent on how much I weigh.	Peace

EVENT	INTERPRETA-TIONS FLIP IT, REFRAMING	EMOTION
My husband does not love me	I am unlovable.	Depression
	I am worthless.	Hopelessness
	Something must be wrong with me.	Failure
	He does not love me but I do.	Confidence
	I can't force anyone to love me.	Freedom
	My friends love me.	Joy Gratitude
	I am lovable.	Happy
Constant problems	Why is life so hard?	Disappointment
	Nothing seems to turn out right.	Hopelessness
	I just feel such a weight.	Despair
	God is unfair.	Anger
	These weighty problems are really exciting challenges.	Hope

	Anything is possible if I don't quit.	Encouragement
	Complaining only brings misery. I will stop complaining for a day.	Peace
	I will quit fixing the blame and fix the problem.	Confidence
No one truly loves me	They all want things from me.	Sadness
	They all take and never give.	Anger
	I must not be lovable.	Depression
	Life is crappy.	Disappointment
	Someone does love me - ME!	Hope
	I am going to treat myself with respect and learn how to nurture myself.	Confidence
	If there are good reasons why people do not treat me right, I am going to change and make necessary improvements.	Determination

EVENT	INTERPRETATIONS FLIP IT, REFRAMING	EMOTION
The dishwasher broke	Why now?	Disappointment
	This has ruined my day!	Anger
	How am I going to pay for it?	Paralyzed
	Nothing ever turns out right.	Hopelessness
	Wow! I got 14 years out of it.	Grateful
	I can always hand wash the dishes.	Determination
	Hey! Dishwashers are on sale this week!	Happiness
I have physical pain	I hate pain!	Disappointment
	Why me?	Trapped
	I'm falling apart.	Hopelessness
	It is what is.	Acceptance
	The doctor may know.	Calm

EVENT	INTERPRETATIONS FLIP IT, REFRAMING	EMOTION
	I can always take a pill.	Okay
	Pain is good. It points to a problem that can hopefully be fixed.	Hope
	I embrace my pain.	Peace
No money to pay the bills.	I will never get financially free.	Hopeless
	Life sucks.	Sadness
	It's all someone else's fault.	Blame
	I will get out of this mess.	Hope
	There is something positive I can do to crawl out of this hole.	Determination
	I'm still alive!	Joy
Traffic mess	I'm going to be late.	Anger
	Why now?	Impatience
	These things happen.	Acceptance

98

	At least I have good music to play.	Hope
	I'm going to be late, but I will make it.	Affirming
	I'm going to smile and relax.	Peace
It's raining again!	This rain is going to spoil our picnic.	Anger
	I hate rain.	Dismayed
	Look at the rainbow!	Surprised
	Rain today, sun tomorrow.	Hopeful
	I accept the rain. We need it.	Grateful
Brother/Sister hates me.	What a miserable family!	Sadness
	Why do other families get along and my family is so dysfunctional?	Hopeless
	I must be the problem.	Distraught
	Though they hate me, I choose to love them and will show that love.	Determination
	I will find out why they hate me.	Honesty

Though some may hate me, I still love myself. And others love me, too!	Joy Gratitude

Do you get the picture? Write out the event, that happening and situation that has you depressed. Then write out your interpretation of that event and then FLIP it.

EVENT + INTERPRETATION = EMOTION

It's that simple. Change your interpretation and you will change how you feel.

Keep playing with this. Come up with an interpretation that is in line with the truth and will make you feel better. **Remember, no EVENT can make you feel bad. It is the INTERPRETATION of that event that is making you feel bad.**

Do this exercise on what you are facing now, the events that have you up in a turmoil. You will be surprised at the insight you are going to have.

EVENT- PRESENT INTERPRETATION / FLIP IT- EMOTION

1.

2.

3.

4.

5.

6.

7.

8.

9.

10.

11.

12.

CHANGE YOUR *INTERPRETATIONS*, AND YOU WILL CHANGE HOW YOU FEEL.

Got it?

It's magical!

SUMMARY: We have seen that events DO NOT equal emotions but our INTERPRETATIONS are what makes us feel bad or good. When we flip and reframe our interpretations we can then change how we feel.

E + I = E really is a magical formula.

More to come!

CHAPTER 5

BREAKTHROUGH FORMULA 3

In the middle of difficulty lies opportunity.
Albert Einstein

Changing your interpretation, "flipping" or reframing it, does wonders. It is incredible what can happen when a person learns how to do this and does it on a regular basis.

It has been decades now since I developed these formulas and used them. Anytime I am feeling bad I go back to the event that I am focused on and change my interpretation.

Bam! I feel better.

STRUGGLE WITH "FLIPPING"

Yet there are times I struggle with coming up with a suitable interpretation. I get fixated on the event so much that I get stuck in it, mired over with negative interpretations that leave me angry, upset and depressed. What do I do to break loose?

Action. I do something counter to the way I'm feeling.

Depressed? I smile or laugh.

Angry? I bless the person I'm angry at, asking God to be good to them.

All the while, I check my breathing. Short breaths mean that I am focusing too much on the event rather than coming up with a right interpretation that will bring relief. In the mean time, I sit in a chair and practice deep breathing. This alone will calm my body and begin to calm my mind to the point where I can flip my interpretation of the event into something that will calm me down and put me back on the road to peace and happiness.

It always is calming to take a walk, breathe the fresh air and notice things in nature, a beautiful tree, a flowering bush, the mountains in the distance, the breeze gracing your face. Any activity like this helps to take away compulsive thinking and getting stuck on a triggering event that has you upset.

You understand how to "flip," or reframe.

Now you are going to focus on another part of this formula.

Action.

ONE BASIC FORMULA TO LEARN

In one sense, I am presenting one formula in this book, but three ways of looking at it.

My basic formula is: **T + A = F**, or Thoughts + Actions = Feelings. The two formulas that follow only help you to better understand my basic formula, T + A = F.

We covered the *ACTION* side of it earlier. I want to impress on you at this time the necessity of using action to break out of your depression. If you are not having success with coming up with interpretations that will quiet your emotional discomfort, then you need to move to the action part of the formula.

Of course, if you work on the entire formula 3 and practice it, I mean REALLY practice it, you will no doubt begin to break through your depression and feel considerably better.

And that's what you want, isn't it? Joy? Happiness? Peace?

Here is Formula 3 written out.

EVENT + INTERPRETATION (THOUGHTS) + *ACTION* = EMOTION

Let me show you how this formula works in a real life situation.

Alex and Sue sat in my office holding hands, yet on the edge of a divorce. I was their last stop before Sue saw her attorney. They had been married 17 years, lived in one of the nicest parts of town, took expensive vacations and had the good life. Or so it seemed.

Alex was CEO of his own company, worked hard and in his free time played golf every chance he could. That meant little time for his family.

Sue was a beautiful woman, artistic, and a great writer. She would often compose a poem for Alex and give it to him as he left for work. One day he took the poem and tore it up in her face and told her he wasn't into that kind of nonsense.

SUE FELT BATTERED, BROKEN, DEPRESSED

You can imagine how Sue felt, emotionally battered, broken, confused and depressed. After years of putting up with this successful jerk, she had had enough. She told him she was leaving him for good.

Alex knew me and gave me a call. He was sobbing. For once he saw the damage he had done to his beautiful wife and family. Up to this point it was all about him - success on the job and on the golf course. Now, he realized what a jerk he had been, an absent father and husband. And he was going to lose it all.

I asked Alex if he and Sue could see me the next day in my office. We set the appointment and they came in and told me the whole story. Though they were holding hands, she was determined to leave. Divorce was the only answer. The hurt and pain were too great. There was no possibility of repair.

As I looked into their eyes, seeing their pain, I also saw their goodness. She had been a fantastic wife and mother. I could see why - her deep desire to be the best. I also saw that Alex, though he had failed miserably in being the kind of husband he could have been, was repentant, broken and willing to start afresh.

So I made a proposition. "If you do what I ask you to do for three months, I believe your marriage can be saved. What I will ask you to do will not be easy. But your 17 year old marriage, I believe, cannot only be saved, but bring joy once again in your lives. Do you have the courage to submit to my guidance? If nothing changes, you can move ahead with the divorce."

At first she was hesitant, and I could understand why. She had experienced so much pain. I wouldn't blame her for seeing her attorney and ending their marriage.

Though hesitant, she and he agreed. They would follow my instructions for three months.

Now I want you to see what I was doing.

For me to ask Sue to change her thoughts would have been almost impossible. "Reinterpret his tearing up your beautiful poems," I could have asked. And, in time, I could have moved her in that direction. We could have come up with an interpretation like: "He hates sentimentality but loves me. He tears up these love notes because they make him feel uneasy." And that interpretation could work.

But then she would have to interpret all the times he neglected her, forgot her birthday and anniversaries. Years of disappointment became so weighty that she could not bear the load.

Ultimately, I could help her to see how to take any event and interpret it in a way where she could feel better.

But not now.

I had to move to action steps. She was going to have to "act herself to a new way of feeling." As I said before, if it is done right, it is not being a phony. You are acting to recover your feelings, good feelings again.

Working with Alex was easy. He was motivated to restore his marriage. Flowers, long times of conversation, asking her to forgive him, as well as asking her what she would like from him.

All of us want to feel significant and secure. So Alex focused on making Sue feel significant, not just by buying her things, but, more importantly, learning how to praise her and tell her how proud he was of her. He began to write notes and place them around the house in unexpected places. He drew up a 30 day plan to help Sue feel important. He came up with some fantastic ideas and put his whole heart and soul into it.

At first she was resistant. "How long would this last," she questioned? Alex had become the kind of husband she dreamed of having. Was it, however, just a show to get her back?

I worked with Sue helping her to take action steps that would ultimately bring back the love feelings. Depression, anger and bitterness kept pushing their way to the surface of her emotions. There was a part of her that wanted him to pay for the way he ignored and insulted her. Yet, to make the three months work, she was going to have to put her heart and soul into it. And Sue was the good kind of person who did her best even though she did not feel like it.

She wrote notes, drew up a list of 20 positive traits about her husband and shared a few with him on various occasions. She hugged and kissed him even though she cringed inside. He had favorite meals which she cooked, rubbed his back, spoke words of love.

But would it work?

She focused almost totally on the ACTION part of the formula. She was resistant to working on changing her interpretations. And I could understand it. That's why I took her to the action part first and went backwards. This would be our only hope for changing her emotions and feelings for Alex.

I saw them separately, each week, over the three month period.

Then one day, I received a call from Sue. "Alex and I would like to meet you at a special steak house. We want you there to make a special announcement," she said with joy in her voice.

When I walked in, Alex and Sue were hand in hand. We sat down, got a few appetizers and ordered our meals. Then Sue said they had a special announcement to make. "I am not going to divorce Alex," she declared as she put her arms around him. Our marriage has been not only saved through your counseling, but we have never been happier. We know now what it takes to make a good and satisfying relationship."

I was fighting back the tears. Three months ago I saw all the pain. Now, the joy and celebration. How did it happen?

Sue decided to ACT in a way she did not feel. She FLIPPED her actions, from actions that encouraged her depression to actions that brought about ultimate joy. In time, the actions began to impact her feelings of depression, hopelessness, anger and bitterness. Through acting, she fell back in love again. Life had a new and fresh glow. FORMULA 3 was working.

EVENT + INTERPRETATION + *ACTION* **= EMOTION**

I think of many others I have had to take down the pathway of ACTIONS first before they were ready to "flip" their interpretations to make them feel better.

LOST JOB

William had lost his job as a sales executive and couldn't seem to find work…for over a year. Depression set in as he felt a deep sense of failure. For him, taking long walks helped to ease the tension and bring back some equilibrium to his life. While walking he would pray and talk with God, pouring out his troubled heart.

One day, while walking, he had a revelation. "Why am I trying to get a sales executive position when I really hate it? Why not do what I enjoy the most…build?"

Within a few months after I saw William, he was willing to begin to reinterpret what had happened to him after first taking some action steps to help him feel better. He realized how stressful his sales position had been, and that he dreamed of doing something else with his life, but never thought it possible. William loved building things around the house. He had built on an extra room, redone the bathrooms and kitchen, and made their home a beautiful place.

William had a breakthrough when he quit fixating on the loss of his job and began to believe that this was for the best. It released him to do what he loved...building. He took out a small business loan and started his own remolding business. It was fantastic!

The pathway to William's recovery was ACTION first, getting off his butt and taking those walks opened the door to rediscovery that led him to see his getting laid off as a blessing and not a curse.

UGLY DIVORCE

Florence had just gone through an ugly divorce that left her emotionally paralyzed. In the process it seemed that everyone was against her, even her children. How could I help this woman trapped in the pits of hopelessness and shame?

At first I worked on Florence's thoughts. But she was resistant. Florence was out to PROVE that all was lost. Nothing would ever be good again. She was stuck, frozen in her state of hopelessness.

I knew that Florence was tied into a good church, and that she had been very involved until the breakup of her marriage.

"Florence, I want you to DO something." Notice I decided to work on the ACTION side of the formula.

"I want you to get out of the house for 2 hours a day. Go to the food bank, Catholic Relief Services or some other service organization and give 2 hours of service at least 3 times a week. Would you do that?"

Florence looked at me for a moment in shock. "I don't feel like doing that."

"Of course you don't feel like doing it," I said. "But, in time, it will have a dramatic affect on your feelings of depression. Will you make a 3 month commitment to do this?"

Florence sat there, head down, thinking. Then she spoke.

"I don't see what good it will do, but I'll do it."

I knew she was going to break out of her depression. This action step was going to be her salvation.

And it did work.

In less than six weeks her moods were beginning to change. The loss of a husband meant the finding of a purpose for her life that dramatically changed how she saw herself and others. For the first time in her life she was learning the beauty of serving others. What an amazing discovery! Florence told me months later that she had never been happier.

ACT YOURSELF TO A NEW WAY OF FEELING

How did this happen? I'm a big believer in reinterpreting events that happen to me. And Florence ultimately had to do this. But she couldn't start there. She had to take ACTION STEPS that had an impact on how she was feeling. She ACTED herself to a new way of feeling - got out of the house and began to give herself to others. That action changed her life.

Let me write out some other events and show you action steps that will help you to feel better. Remember. Though you will not feel like taking these action steps, taking them will actually make you feel better. You are not just trying to "fake it to feel it," but rather to "faith it to feel it." This is an act of faith, believing that your good and healthy action will bring about a change in your emotions.

As you focus on your actions, be aware of the action steps you are presently taking that aid in your depression: lack of laughter and smiling, shallow breathing, little exercise, not doing positive things for others, bent over, looking down, shuffling in your walk instead of walking with your head back with determined steps, sitting instead of serving others, crying instead of laughing to name a few.

Changing your action is not easy. It takes determination. You have to FORCE yourself to do this. Yet, in this forceful action, you will actually begin to feel better.

Remember: When you connect this action with a change of your interpretation, it's powerful!

EVENT	ACTION	EMOTION
LOST JOB	Smile	Hopeful
	Look for job	Determination
	Focus on heart's desires for job	Excitement
	Laugh/Dance	Joy
	Relax/Deep breaths	Peace
	Go for a walk	Calm
HUSBAND IS A JERK	Write out his 20 positive attributes and share them with him	Caring
	Write out a list of 10 ways you can please him and do them one at a time	Determination
	Smile/Laugh/Dance	Joy
	Focus on fun with girlfriends	Anticipation
	Counter his jerkiness with love	Brave
	Give a blessing for a curse	Love
NEWS IS BAD	Turn off the news	Less anxiety
	Play uplifting music	Joy
	Focus on the good news	Hopeful
	Google good news	Inspired
	Turn on the radio and listen to music	Calming

EVENT	ACTION	EMOTION
EVERYTHING'S BAD	Put a big smile on your face	Gratefulness
	Laugh for one minute. Do this 10 times today	Pleasure
	Write out a list of people you can do something for that would make them happy	Happy
	Doing good deeds plus anticipation equals…	Joy!
CANCER	Smile. Say: "I've got cancer but cancer doesn't have me!"	Determination
	Cry (It is never good to repress actions that flow from a terrible event. Grief, anger, anxiety, depression, loneliness and other emotional responses are healthy. They become UNHEALTHY, though when we hang on to them for an extended period of time. You must be honest and truthful in your approach to writing out interpretations and actions)	Release anxiety
	Shout: "I'm going to win! Cancer is going to lose!"	Hope

EVENT	ACTION	EMOTION
	Laugh	Daring
	Write a list of things and people you are grateful for	Thanksgiving
	Become part of a support group	Encouragement
INVESTMENT DOWN	Practice deep breathing	Peace
	Smile	Joy
	Laugh	Optimistic
	Shout: "I'm down but not out!"	Hopeful
	Go for a walk	Calming
HUSBAND LEFT	Cry	Release tension
	Say: "Something good will happen."	Hopeful
	Smile	Joy
	Laugh for a minute 10 times a day	Bold, giddy
	Get a dog, cat, bird	Energized, love
	See your pastor/ counselor	Focused
	Go out to eat with a friend	Supportive
PROBLEMS WITH FAMILY, WORK, FRIENDS, MOTHER, HEALTH	Stop complaining!	Relaxed

EVENT	ACTION	EMOTION
	Get off your butt and do something!	Determination
	Write out a list of your problems and what you plan on DOING about it	Hopeful
	Quite bitching and start blessing	Joyful
	Focus on blessing	Gratefulness
	Write out a list of all the good things about your family, work, friends, mother, health, etc.	Positive
	Smile, laugh, breathe, shout, dance	Liberated
	Walk, eat good foods for your brain (omega 3), build strong social networks, walk, workout, listen to music	All these things bring a calm to the brain and peace to the soul
FLAT TIRE	Say: "Thank God I have a spare!"	Joy
	Smile/Laugh	Excitement
	Stop complaining!	Peace
HUSBAND DIED	Cry	Release tension
	Smile	Gratefulness
	Say: " Thank God he isn't suffering anymore."	Thankful

EVENT	ACTION	EMOTION
	List all the good attributes he had	Grateful
	Say: "I will make it."	Determination
	Buy a bird, dog, cat, fish	Fills up that lonely space
	Be with family/friends	Calm
SOMEONE HATES ME	Smile	Joy
	List 10 positive characteristics about yourself	Hope
	List all the people who love you	Peace
	Write out ways you can love those who hate or dislike you	Determination
	Eat foods rich in omega 3 fats	Feeds the brain and makes it feel better

EVENT	ACTION	EMOTION
TIRED	Breathe	Peace
	Smile	Joy
	Take a nap	Hope
	Go for a slow walk	Energizes
	Eat foods that give energy	Determination

You get the idea, don't you? We will go into more detail in Book 2, but before you go there, work on the ACTION part. Then put both the action and interpretation part together.

CHANGE YOUR *INTERPRETATION* AND *ACTION* and you will feel better...a whole lot better. You will break down the bars of your prison and be set free!

HALLELUJAH!

Practice this on the events and situations you face. List your situation and the action step you can take and the feeling you hope to receive. You should also be aware of the action you are now exhibiting like shallow breaths, frowning, complaining, looking down, isolated, listing all that is bad, ungratefulness, etc.

EVENT………ACTION………EMOTION

1.

2.

3.

4.

5.

6.

7.

8.

9.

10.

11.

12.

13.

14.

15.

16.

17.

T + A = F

We started with T + A = F and have come full circle. Thoughts about triggering events that happen and our interpretations of them plus action will produce either good or bad feelings. It all depends how we interpret and act.

It's that simple. And it works!

Mary, the mother who lost her daughter, got breast cancer and had a husband who left her for another woman, all happening in three difficult, depressing years, finally got it. After eight weeks of therapy, she learned how to change her interpretations about the sad and tragic events that happened to her.

She was able to:

- Take her daughter's death and focus not on the death, but the life of her daughter.
- Take her breast cancer and instead of morn the loss of her breasts, focus on a life that God gave her now.
- Discover that a woman's worth is not to be found in a part of her body, but in WHO she was and is.

Last, when her husband left her for another woman she was devastated. The loneliness and rejection she felt was almost unbearable. Mary had so many questions about why all these things occurred to her in such a short time - 3 years of hell.

But as Mary began to change her interpretations, she began to find new life. Did her husband define who she was? No. Mary was a beautiful person no matter what happened to her. And she began to let that beauty out by engaging in activities at her church and getting involved with a hospice group where she could bring hope and peace to others who were suffering. Mary got OUTSIDE OF HERSELF and began to focus on OTHERS.

And her life radically changed.

Yes, there were those tragic events that happened to her, but she took those lemons and made lemonade; she changed her sour interpretations about life and made life sweet once again.

This can happen to you. This WILL happen to you if only…

If only you will take these three formulas and put them into practice.

You only have your depression to lose!

SUMMARY OF THE BOOK:

FORMULA 1
THOUGHTS + ACTIONS = FEELINGS

Remember, your feelings are held captive by what you think and what you do. Change your thoughts and actions and you are guaranteed to feel better.

FORMULA 2

EVENT + INTERPRETATION = EMOTIONS

This formula helps you understand how your thoughts work. Thoughts are always made up of your INTERPRETATIONS. Events do not create your feelings, your interpretations do. Change your interpretations and you will change your feelings.

FORMULA 3

EVENT + INTERPRETATIONS + *ACTIONS* = EMOTIONS

This formula combines it all. It shows that sometimes it's hard to focus on interpretations at first. So you approach the changing of your emotions in a different way, focusing on ACTIONS instead, realizing that in time you have to deal with your interpretations.

Now take your events, those triggering situations and fill out a healing approach so that you can feel good again. Write down both the interpretations and action you are taking, the kind that are making you feel bad. Then, FLIP those interpretations and actions. Take the time to do this.

The results will be thrilling!

EVENT	INTERPRETA-TION...FLIP... REFRAME	ACTION/FLIP	EMOTION

Congratulations for completing this assignment.

The more you work on your interpretations, seeing what they are and flipping them, then adding appropriate actions, the better you will get at doing this. Soon, you will be automatically coming up with interpretations and actions that will make you feel better, interpretations and actions based on what is true.

These concepts I have taught you are not always easy to learn. Thoughts develop grooves in the brain, and repeated thoughts and interpretations can dig a channel that is hard to break loose from.

So I have developed a two special programs to help you do this.

1. A workbook based on Book 1 called *10 DAYS TO A NEW LIFE*. This is an especially designed, turbo-charged program to help you take what you read in Book 1 and put it into practice within 10 days.

2. Next is my proprietary *QUICK RELIEF* **YES!** cards. These are PRESCRIPTIONS for your inward soul that will help you break loose from your depression. You can download these cards to any android device, an I-Phone, or computer. I

recommend you putting them on a phone you carry around with you.

These *QUICK RELIEF* cards are part of my **TOTAL RELIEF SYSTEMS**.

You have often heard that, "Practice makes perfect." Well, these flash cards and assignments will assist you in learning how to take the events that happen to you, change your interpretations and actions in a way will set you free from your depression, and replace it with bounding joy.

There are sufficient cards that are designed to do this - targeted help with directions included so you can get the most from these cards.

The cost, of course, is minimal. Patients have paid me hundreds of dollars to learn how to use them. You will pay less than a cup of coffee!

I encourage you to download them and perfect what I have given you in Book 1 - the three formulas. Working on your thoughts and actions will lay a great foundation for the next book in my series on TOTAL RELIEF.

These can be downloaded from amazon.com or download them at the end of this book.

As I prayed for Mary who was suffering from such horrendous depression, I also am praying for you that you will break out of this horrible prison, be set free and find the life of your dreams.

In closing, what I have shared with you is cognitive-behavioral therapy in a very simple manner. Too often, therapy stops at this point and doesn't take a person deeper to the point where they can overcome depression for good.

My next two books will do that for you.

Book 2 will take you a lot deeper into understanding why you may have trouble changing your interpretations. I have found that these three formulas I gave you, give insight to many and help them break free from their depression and other emotional issues.

But too often these three formulas fell short in bringing TOTAL RELIEF. More help was needed.

So in my next book you will get other formulas that will give you a lot more insight and help you to form better interpretations about the events, happenings, and situations in your life.

Some of you, right now, are facing difficult and heart wrenching situations. Why are you going through this? What can you do to break loose from your depression and hopelessness? Formula 1, 2 & 3 are of great help. But FORMULA 4, 5 and 6 in Book 2 will give you a foundation to where, no matter what happens, you can live that joyful and fulfilled life you desire.

But before you download Book 2, be sure and download the workbook for Book 1, *10 DAYS TO A NEW LIFE*. The download my *QUICK RELIEF* YES! cards. You will be glad you did. In fact, it will bring gladness and joy into your life, the kind that you dream about.

Remember: It is too often easier to FIX THE BLAME rather than FIX THE PROBLEM. Anyone can focus on the events that have happened to them and sit mired in darkness and hopelessness. It takes courage to move from fixing the blame to fixing the problem. And when you do, you only have your depression to lose!

So let's together move and FIX THE PROBLEM. Work at changing your thoughts and actions and you will begin to enter into a brand new life.

Go for it!

APPENDIX A

THE THREE BREAKTHROUGH FORMULAS

1. FORMULA 1

THOUGHTS + ACTION = FEELINGS

2. FORMULA 2

EVENTS + *INTERPRETATION* = EMOTION

3. FORMULA 3

EVENTS + INTERPRETATION + *ACTION* = EMOTIONS

TESTING YOUR KNOWLEDGE

1. What is FORMULA 1? How do thoughts and actions break us out of the prison of depression?

2. What is FORMULA 2? How does this make formula 1 so effective? Interpretations are thoughts focused on seeking to understand events, happenings and situations. How does changing your interpretations change how you feel? Illustrate it from your own life. Downloading the TOTAL RELIEF SYSTEM cards will help you come up with interpretations that will smash your depressions.

3. What is FORMULA 3? What does this formula add to formula 2? How do actions help in changing your feelings?

APPENDIX B

A DESCRIPTION OF THE VARIOUS FORMS OF THERAPY FOR DEPRESSION. WHY MY BREAKTHROUGH FORMULAS ARE SUPERIOR

The various forms used to treat depression are:

1. **Psychotherapy.** It is always good to talk with a qualified health professional, but getting to the source of your problems may take months or years. For most people suffering from depression, this approach is not the best because of the amount of time it takes and the tedious digging around in one's past can do more harm than good. Remember, it is not your past that is creating your emotional problems but your present thoughts. Psychotherapy that is cognitive based is by far the best.

2. **Medications.** These are used to release serotonin in one's brain, a chemical that helps to overcome depression. This is obviously a good thing, but there are side affects like dry mouth, headaches, dizziness, drowsiness, problems with skin, eyes, ears and sexual side effects as well as nervousness and sleep problems. It must be noted that there can be a dependency on the drug to do what the patient should be learning to do for themselves. There are also alternative types of medications like St. Johns Wart, a product you can get at a health food store. Of course, always talk to your doctor before you start or stop any medications or take anything else.

3. **Exercise.** This can naturally increase levels of serotonin that can help reduce depression. Walking is one of the best exercises for depression because it gets you outdoors, breathing fresh air, and has the potential of putting your mind on something else besides your problems. **It has been shown that 30 minutes of exercise done three times a week is as good as antidepressants in beating mild to moderate depression** (Study done at Duke University).

4. **Diet.** Foods that are rich in omega 3 (including fish and fish oil), can help, plus reducing sugar, along with eating a good, balanced diet. If you change what goes into your body, you can often change what goes on with your brain. Food is a chemical and can have an impact on your thoughts both good and bad.

5. **Hospitalization.** Suicidal attempts must be treated immediately. Sometimes intervention is required.

6. **Electroshock.** Can stimulate the production of serotonin that reduces depression.

7. **Hypnosis.** Some are helped in this relaxed state where new thoughts are implanted that will help one to change one's thinking and actions (posture, breathing, etc.).

8. **Acupuncture.** A recent study showed that this can be as good or better than medications and produces fewer side effects. As with all alternative approaches to depression, studies continue.

9. **Mechanical devices** like the *Fisher Wallace Stimulator* show promise for treating depression, insomnia, anxiety and pain. It is my belief that though these products will bring relief to many, they are not designed to bring TOTAL RELIEF. They deal with the chemistry in the brain but do not deal with the emptiness of the heart.

10. **COGNITIVE-BEHAVIORAL THERAPY.** *This, I believe, has been proven to be one of the best, if not the best approach to treat depression.* Test after test reveals that it is on the par with medicine without the side affects. And in the long run, it is superior because people learn how to change their lives rather than rely on chemicals to change their thoughts and behavior.

Cognitive-behavioral therapy has been shown to actually change the chemistry of the brain!

Of course, always check with your doctor before you plan on making a change.

APPENDIX C

The power of positive thinking and using affirmations to rid depression.
Why these approaches often do not work.

It is not that positive thinking and using affirmations are bad. The problem arises when they are not based on what is true. Repeating 1,000 times, "I am not depressed," will not work if you do not get to the root of your depression and treat it in a truthful way. Saying, "I'm so happy," ten times an hour will not help to make you happy if you do not understand what is making you sad and depressed.

Didn't Jesus say: "...the TRUTH will set you free?"

When we cover our problems with affirmations and positive thinking that are not aligned with the truth, we will never fully recover from depression.

This is why Book 2 is so important. It will help you to see what is fundamentally, and absolutely true. It is then that you can scrape off the exterior affirmations that you have been painting over your depression, hoping to get rid of it. **You need to get rid of the dry rot that is ultimately causing your depression to make you a whole person again, not by saying just positive things or quoting awesome affirmations.**

What will happen to you will be positive, and there will be TRUTHFUL affirmations that you will be able to say. However, the gunk, the stuff that is making you depressed, will be rooted out FIRST so that you can experience TOTAL RELIEF.

And that's what its all about, isn't it?

That's what you desperately want.

And it's yours. So keep on moving on with my TOTAL RELIEF program! You will not only lose your depression but gain a totally new and exciting life!

Dr. Paul

Education:

University of California, Fresno, B.A in English

Dallas Theological Seminary, Th.M (Masters in Theology)

Biola University, Doctorate of Ministry with emphasis on psychology (working with Talbot School of Theology, Rosemead School of Psychology and other schools)

Dr. Paul Joseph Young helped grow one of the largest churches in the Dallas/Ft. Worth area as its pastor, working with thousands of people, developing his skills both as a minister, communicator and a counselor. For seven years he was C.E.O. of Community Bible Study International, working in over 60 countries of the world.

Dr. Paul's communication skills have made him a favorite speaker around the world. He lives with his wife Diane. They have five children and 14 grandchildren.

More than anything, Dr. Paul lives to help people find the joyful life they deserve.

OTHER BOOKS BY DR. PAUL

1. **TOTAL RELIEF SYSTEMS SERIES.** These are books written to help people overcome their emotional struggles and find peace, purpose, and joy.
   - Depression
   - Worry and Anxiety
   - Stress
   - Anger
   - Loneliness
   - Fear
   - Inferiority
   - Grief
   - Others

2. **The Personalized Bible**, Philippians

   This book will help you to make right choices about feeling great. I take the book of Philippians, a book in the New Testament, and write it as if it were written to YOU. If you read it for 30 days in a row, this book could have a great impact the joy you experience every day.

3. **If there a God, Whose God is God?**
Belief is based not on a "hope so" feeling, but on facts, facts that give assurance that brings hope.

4. **Dr. Paul's Encyclopedia of Triggering Events** and how to use them to feel great. In this book you can find the events you blame for your depression and see how to reinterpret them so you come out feeling great.

5. **Lethal Discord,** a Catholic Thriller. This has been called a "page turner" by many who read it. You will love the story and learn about your faith as you read this compelling novel.

6. **Lethal Discord companion guide** with questions that will help you dig deeper into the novel.

7. **Great Men of the Bible** - Saint Paul, his secret to success. The story of his success can be yours!

8. **Great Women of the Bible** - women you never knew before. This is an inspiring tale of three great women in the bible and how they overcame difficulty.

9. **How to Pray the Rosary for your Family** - how to take each mystery and apply them to your family in a powerful program that could change you and your family

10. **Know What You Believe** - the catechism for today. A simple way to learn what you believe, a method for yourself and your family.

11. **You Can Change Your World** - a powerful book that gives us the secret to changing our world

12. **How To Finish Well.** A Catholic book for Retired Men

13. **Potato Salad for the Depressed Soul** - Magical steps to take to blast away depression while making potato salad!

14. **How To Be An IMPACT MAN**...in your family, work, church and beyond. This book is going to start a spiritual revolution among men. Finally there is a path they can take that will make them the man that God desires.

15. **The NOTE.** A visual and verbal parable of hope and joy. This book will help you to experience the meaning of life that will deeply move your soul.

You can find other books written by Dr. Paul J. Young on:

DrPaulPress.com

This is a **TOTAL RELIEF** *SYSTEMS* publication

My prayer for you:

May you break down the prison bars of your depression

May you learn that you don't have to be weighed down

    Heavy

    Hopeless

    Angry

    Alone.

May you experience the fullness of who you were meant
  to be

    Bold

    Engaged

    Alive

    Filled with happiness

    Overflowing

    With exploding joy!

May God grant you the desires of your heart.

    Amen

I've made an appointment to see you in BOOK 2

I am going to take you a lot deeper, drilling down to the foundation of your thoughts so that you can be more affective in interpreting every event that happens to you and come out feeling good.

BEFORE you get BOOK 2, work through the workbook designed for Book 1, **10 DAYS TO A NEW YOU**. Then download the QUICK RELIEF, **YES!** cards. You can order them on amazon.com. These additional products will insure that you get the most out of BOOK 1.

Then move on to...

Dr. Paul's
TOTAL RELIEF

Book 2
DEPRESSION

Covering additional, healing formulas

BREAKTHROUGH formulas that will liberate you

More than you'd ever imagine!

I would appreciate if you would **give me a good review of this book.** A good review (5 stars) encourages people to read the book and hopefully change their lives. Thank you for taking the time to do this. Go to this book title where you bought it at amazon.com.

A **DrPaulPress.com** publication

Products that make a difference now...and forever

Made in the USA
San Bernardino, CA
19 November 2015